# PASSIVE INCOME PLANNER 2015

## How to make passive income 2015

*Vindimear D Heart*

# Passive Income Planner 2015

### Vindimear D Heart

# Passive Income Planner 2015

Copyright © 2015 by Vindimear D Heart

# Table of Contents

# Introduction

Thank you for downloading the book "Passive Income Planner 2015." This book is a compilation of easy ways to create passive income that you can all do, in any order you prefer, in six months.

Each chapter discusses in detail a specific, easy way to generate income. You will be given tips and techniques that will allow you to successfully start a passive income stream. Thanks again for downloading this book, I hope you enjoy it!

# Chapter 1:   Sell Information Products

A new year is soon coming. 2015 is just around the corner and you should definitely think of ways of how you could earn more.

The thing is that it's only not earning more that you should think about. You should also be concerned about the state of your health and your happiness, too! And that's why this 2015, you should learn how to earn passive income!
There are actually various ways of earning passive income but it's best if you focus on one thing alone, especially when you're just starting, and see where that leads you. With that in mind, why don't you try selling information products?
What are they?

Information Products are basically products that help people become knowledgeable about certain topics or subjects. They could either be DVD's, CD's, E-books, or manuals. What matters is that they make it easy for others to learn more about what they want to learn.

Some examples include Exercise Tutorials on DVD, Cookbooks, Diet Plans, books that talk about home organization or how to clean one's house, and products that show how some items work. Information Products are around because they're meant to make life easier for most people so when people buy them, they have to be assured that they'll really learn something.

But, since competition is tough everywhere, you have to be sure that you get to create some of the best products so that once they become available to the public, you can be sure that they'd want to try them and you won't be too stressed out about it. That way, you can also be sure that you're getting the right kind of passive income!

Only the Best
So, how exactly can you come up with the best information products that aren't available anywhere else? There are a couple of reasons to do this and they are as follows:

·      Make sure that you produce valuable content. It all begins with an idea. Think about what people would want to watch or read. What are they concerned about? What do they want to know more about? For example, these days, most people are concerned about the state of their health, so you can make information products about new diet programs or exercise regimens, or supplements that they can take. Focus on one idea alone so everything will be cohesive.

·      Choose your target demographic. It would also be extremely helpful if you know who your target demographic is. While you may think that getting passive income is about being popular to all demographics, you also have to keep in mind that once you have a target audience and you get to their heart, it'll be easy for them to understand where you're coming from and to appreciate what you have made. Then, you can take it from there.

- Make sure that you understand your audience. Sure, you're giving them information products. Sure, you want to teach them something, but you also have to be sure that you get through to them and that you give them what they need and want. After all, if you don't know what your customers want, and if you can't make them happy then you can also expect that your business might falter. Even some of the most popular passive income businessmen such as Marcus Buckingham and Tony Robbins made sure that they knew exactly what their audience wanted—and that's why they became successful.

- Know the costs. In any business, it is clearly very important that one takes care of the finances and that one knows exactly how much money will be used in making various information products. Never start anything without putting out a business plan and without thinking about the finances so you won't burn a hole in your pocket and you won't feel trapped.

- Test your products. It's just right that before you put out your products in the market, you have to make sure that they work first. This means that you have to try them out, test them, and see whether they're of great quality already or if you have to get some things changed. The earlier you spot the problems, the better.

·     Start Small. Have you ever heard of the saying that every great thing came from small beginnings? Well, that's true. If you feel like you have no idea where to start or who to sell your products to, why don't you start with the people around you? Tell your family and friends about them, send messages to people on your e-mail list, and send text messages, too. Sure, some people might be annoyed, but there will always be people who'll be interested in what you have to say—so focus on that.

·     And, make sure that your products stand out. Do lots of research. Don't copy what's already out there—make products that are uniquely yours. Think about what's missing; think about what people need. Once you take these things into consideration, you'll certainly be able to make products that people will use and will be happy with.

Keep these tips in mind and you'll certainly be able to gain passive income without any hassle. Good Luck!

# Chapter 2:  Blogging for Passive Income

2014 is almost over. This means that you have to start thinking of ways on how you can make 2015 a better year, and better usually means that you will no longer feel like you don't have enough money to buy what you need, and that you'd also have an ample amount of money to buy what you want.

There may be times when you'd feel like your business, or your job, or whatever it is that you're doing right now is no longer enough for you. That's when the need to gain passive income comes in!

Passive income means that you can be paid even if you're just in the comforts of your own home. This means that you no longer have to work in the office day in and day out, and that you get to be more creative with what you're doing. But, even if the word "passive" is in it, it does not necessarily mean that you'll just sit there and do nothing. There are also times when you have to get your brain working—but you need not worry about it much because this is definitely way more fun than what you usually do.

# All for the Blog

One of the ways of gaining passive income is blogging. Yes, you read that one right. Imagine, just by sitting down in front of your computer, writing some content, and waiting for people to check out your blog, you'd already be gaining loads of cash!

One prime example of this is British Blogger Zoe Sugg, more popularly known as "Zoella", started blogging about beauty products, her own beauty regimen, and mostly everything under the sun back in 2009. Since then, she has gained millions of followers on her blog, went on to YouTube and became a popular video blogger, and even landed her a book deal, and was able to make her own beauty line, too! So, how can you be sure that you become that successful, too? How can you make your blog work for you? Here are some suggestions.

·    Make it a consultation blog. Some of the most successful bloggers are those who allowed their readers to interact with them by means of consultation. Basically, these are people who are knowledgeable about certain subjects and they let their expertise lead them to the top. Examples include SOSFactory.com's Sergio, who is a popular web designer, and Twitterpreneu.com's Maren Kate, whose blog is technically an online PR Firm.

·     Make a membership website. Membership websites are basically blogs that ask their readers to pay minimal membership fees, then talk about the blog to others so others would sign up, too, then eventually, they'll all get paid. Of course, the more members a blog has, the better, because it means that the payment will be higher. Everyone wants money. Everyone wants to get paid, and that's why if you do this to your blog, you can be sure that you'll definitely gain lots of traffic and people will be interested in what you have to say. Some of the best examples are LearningIndonesian.com, and Self Starter's Weekly Tips.

·     Sell Courses. Aside from allowing people to consult you about certain things, you can also make your blog something of an online school by selling courses. This way, once people read your content and subscribe to your blog, they'll get the chance to take hold of manuals or Audio-Video courses about various topics such as cooking, guitar lessons, language lessons, and the like.

· Put samples of your book on the blog. You know how people have very low attention span these days, right? More often than not, they won't just buy a book without knowing what it's about first. There are also times when it's okay for them to read excerpts from the book before they decide to buy the book in full. This way, when they visit your blog and get to read what you have written, they'll be excited to read the rest of it so of course, they'd buy from you. Voila! Passive income will then be in your hands. Some prime examples of people who do this are Darren Rowse of Problogger, Ramit Sethi of Iwillteachyoutoberich, and JD Roth of Getrichslowly.com.

· Innovate. You know what's great about the internet? You can make your own rules! You can put something that hasn't been there before. You can get people's attention simply by being different. Iwearyourshit.com is a prime example of this. Basically, the owners of the blog wear the company t-shirts of various business and they get paid to do this. Why? Because it's a form of advertising! And these days, people will do everything they can to advertise!

· Make use of your expertise. And, most importantly, make use of your brains and what you know best. Zoella became her own beauty expert. Maybe, you're great when it comes to cleaning the house. Why not make your own cleaning house blog? Why not give tips about what you know best? This way, people will really listen to you and you'll get paid by advertisers, too!

You want passive income? Turn on your computer, make your own blog, and start writing now!

# Chapter 3:   More Passive Income Ideas

In the coming year, you have to make sure that one of your goals is to be financially stable. Aside from your job, you can also earn more during the weekends or on your free time by means of trying out some passive income businesses.

You know, there are actually people who leave their jobs for this, especially if they feel stable already, or if they feel like their jobs are not making them grow anymore. However, you can choose to do this and your job, too, especially if you know you can—or you can also just take a leap of faith and try passive income businesses and see where they lead you!

## Try these out

In 2015, most passive income businesses will be on the rise and if you're not ready for them, and then you'd probably have a hard time because you won't be able to keep track of what's new in the line of business. Needless to say, if you really want to earn more then you have to open your mind to what's currently on the rise.

So, what are these businesses? What are you going to do with them, and how can you try them out? Here are some ideas:

·      Dividend Stock Investing. Dividend Stock Investing is mainly about investing some money and watching their value grow overtime. Basically, what you have to do is choose stocks that you think have the most potential of growing and will be able to pay you an ample amount of cash each quarter, which is known as the dividend payment, then passive income comes because you'd pretty much just wait for the stocks to grow as a shareholder and you'll already get paid!

·      Take Paid Surveys. There are so many survey websites online. In fact, you may already have come across some of them but you just dismissed them because they annoyed you or because you don't think that they're worth your time. But, come to think of it, you'd lose nothing if you sign up. You probably waste time on so many websites so already so what's another one? Imagine, just by completing surveys and sharing them with others or recommending others to answer them, too, you'd already be given some money! That's not so bad, is it? All you have to have is an opinion and you're all set.

· Earn Royalties. Some people want to get published, and some others want to make their way into the music scene but realistically speaking, everyone knows that competition is tough so sometimes, you have to be content with what you can do in the moment. This does not mean that you have to kill your dreams—it only means that you can still do them, but be willing to let others take credit. It's not wrong because someday, you can still put yourself out there. You see, by means of ghostwriting, or bidding on songs, you can get royalties and may even get paid each month. Now, that's something great because at least, you can save up for the future and sooner or later, you can create more of your own books and songs, too!

· Multi-Level Marketing. You know what the problem with multi-level marketing is? Some people dismiss it as just another scam or a pyramid gimmick. The thing is, it's different than that in such a way that when you try multi-level marketing, you don't just ask people to invest some money and you don't just recruit them for nothing—you're actually letting them sign up for a business where they get to sell products and services. And that is one clear sign that it's a legit business and you'll definitely get paid.

· Try Affiliate Marketing. You've probably already heard about affiliate marketing as a means to gain passive income. Well, it's popular because it's true and it really does work. Affiliate Marketing is basically about signing up on a website and selling this website's products and services. You can make use of your e-mail account or social media profiles to market the products and you'd earn thousands of dollars in a month alone!

· Peer-to-Peer Lending. More commonly known as P2P, it's about loaning people money and deciding how much interest you'll put on it. In fact, you can gain up to 20% of interest—which definitely is a great thing! Check out some prospect candidates for loans online and see what you can do with them.

· Bond Interests. If you feel like stocks are too risky and that you just don't want to try them out, why not make use of bond interests instead? It's a given fact that bonds are more stable and they'll provide you with better returns. It's like, you'll see yourself as a loaner and you get to collect the interests of debt payment, which everyone knows is a big deal so you might as well try this out.

It's an ever-changing world and the earning passive income is one of those signs that this world is no longer as it once was. Take note of these tips, see what you can do, and remember that there's no harm in trying. Good Luck!

# Chapter 4: Passive Income Tips

Earning Passive Income has recently been gaining the curiosity of many. Some people think that by just sitting there, they'd already get paid. But those who know the niche will tell you that it's not merely just a "sit down and get rich" kind of thing—it also requires a whole lot of dedication.
Why is that so? Well, you can come to think of the fact that whatever kind of job you have, as long as it's legal, it's still a job so you have to put your heart and soul into it. Someone who put a lot of passion and dedication to gain passive income is Pat Flynn, a former Architecture Firm employee who created his own website and let Google AdSense posts ads into it. With just three clicks, he already gained more than a dollar, and then eventually, he earned around $30 each day. In a matter of a month, he had earnings of over $7,000! Now, he also has two sites, namely Smart Passive Income Podcast and Smart Passive Income so he gets paid even more!

## What to do

The problem is most people is that they want to earn a hundred dollars right away in one day alone—and that's just not possible unless you actually work hard, put yourself out there, and became known in whatever niche you're in. But, you can always start small like Pat Flynn, and make sure that you're on your way to the top—slowly but surely.
Do you want to earn a lot of money, too? Well, you can do so—but first, you have to keep these tips in mind:

· Decide that you want to do this. It all starts with a decision. It all starts with you knowing that you're actually ready for this and that no one pressured you to do this because that's the only way for you to feel like you can be good at this.

· Ask yourself why exactly you want to do this. Of course, everyone wants a hefty sum of cash—but are you doing this just for the money? Or, do you have other plans and other reasons in mind? Yes, getting paid is a goal and it could motivate you—but you also have to keep in mind that work isn't all about the money, it's also about showing what you can give. It's also about knowing what people need and want so you can give it to them. Once you put that in mind, you'll be more motivated to do your best.

· Choose your platform. So, where do you actually want to put up your online business? Think about it. Are you going to create a blog or your own website? Do you want to make use of social networking sites as means for marketing your services more? You have to choose your main platform before choosing marketing routes so that people will see that you're serious about this and that you're a professional.

· Work on it every day. The most successful people in life are those who didn't give up right away. They're the ones who worked hard each and every single day because they know that with time comes improvement and that if you work hard every day, you'd get to learn more and you'd be more fulfilled. Don't ever think that once you have set up your website and put yourself out there then you have to do nothing anymore. Passive Income is not like that, you know?

· Find your niche. So, maybe, forex trading is all the rage these days. Some others also sell information products about cooking or exercises. It might be practical to join those niches, too, but you know that if you're not that knowledgeable about those things then you might not be able to give your customers what they really want. It's always good to focus on what you know best then while you're there, you can study about other niches so you can decide whether you want to dive into those to or not.

· Ask for feedback. Whatever it is that you're selling or putting up on the web, you should never forget to ask for honest feedback. Sure, it may be scary as some people may be a little too critical and may denounce your works, but you know, it's the only way for you to learn whether or not your products or services are actually great or if there's a lot of work to do about them. Listen to what your customers say because in the end, they're the ones who can make or break your business.

· Keep improving. Learn more about what people want. Think about what's best for the world today. Keep improving because times change—everything changes, actually, and you have to learn how to ride change.

· And, give it time. Again, riches don't come overnight. You have to make sure that you are patient enough and that you give it time, or else nothing will happen. That's the key to success in any kind of business.

A great future awaits you—but you have to make sure that you're ready for it and that you're willing to be the best that you can be. Once you decide to do so, passive income will certainly be yours!

## Chapter 5: Passive Income through Investing

So, you're willing to invest in forex trading or stocks. You might even be willing to go for bond interests. But are you sure that you already know what to do?

Basically, when you choose to invest, you can also expect that you'll get paid after a certain span of time. But since money is involved, you shouldn't just shelve out some cash without thinking of what could happen. And that's why you need to be educated about these things. You have to be sure that you're doing the right thing and that you're on the right track.

Everyone wants to experience earning passive income but the thing is, not everyone is aware of what should be done, and how they should go forth with the whole business of investing. Well, if you're one of those people, fear no more. With the help of this article, you'll learn everything you need to know about how investing can help you gain passive income and what you should do with it. Read on and find out.

# FAQ's

Q: Who can invest?
A: As long as anyone is of legal age (21 years of age), he can invest and expect that he'll gain passive income. It also does not matter if he wants to invest as an individual, or as part of a partnership or company, as long as he presents proper identification and documents needed by the firm that he is investing in.

Q: What's usually the minimum amount for investment?
A: Well, this varies from time to time, depending on the firm and on the agreement, but more often than not, you can start investing when you already have $5000 to $10,000 on hand. You can add more, provided that you'll be ready to add increments of thousands.

Q: What other fees should I pay?
A: Again, this varies depending on your partners or the firm, but more often than not, you may have to pay a performance fee, which is 20% of what you have invested, 1.98% of yearly management fee to make sure that your funds are being taken care of and that everyone gets to be paid, and around 4% of contribution fee, which makes you an official part of the firm.
Some other firms may ask you to pay more or less, so you definitely have to check with them first because it's really different for everyone.

**Q:** When can I expect the distributions to be paid?
**A:** There are often two types of distributions. The first one happens twice a year, mostly in June and December, while the other one happens Quarterly, or in April, August, and December.

You can also take the distributions as cash or dividends that you can choose to reinvest. This can be determined by what you and the firm agreed upon during the signing of the contract, but in case you change your mind and make another decision, make sure that you let the firm or your partners know so proper changes could be made.

You'll also know if it's already the time for distributions because you will be notified and you'll also get a Taxation Distribution Statement so you could also take note of your tax returns. These statements come annually so please wait for them and never take them for granted.

**Q:** How much would I be paid?
**A:** This depends on the firm and on the implications of taxes and it's usually chartered accountants who get to calculate this. But, one thing's for sure: As long as you have invested, you can expect that you'll get paid on the distribution period that you and the firm have agreed upon.

Q: What price will these units be in?

A: Usually, unit price can be determined by means of dividing the fund's net tangible assets by how many units have been issued. This will be known by the end of the business month. However, some firms choose to determine this when it's the 12th of the month, or the 3rd Friday of the month, so you can also say that it varies.

Q: What if I want to transfer or sell my units?

A: If you come to the realization that you want your units transferred, you immediately have to notify the firm then ask for a Transfer Notification Form so that you can fill it up right away and get the changes done.

However, when it comes to selling your units, you have to keep in mind that this isn't always possible and that more often than not, the firm will just buy those units back. The price that you'd have to pay is the price that was determined in the month before you have made the redemption request.

Q: Is it okay to call my partners, or the place I have invested in if I have any questions?

A: Of course, it is. It's your money so it's your right to know what happens to it.

## Learn More

You see, you can always learn about passive income. It may seem complicated at first, but once you get the hang of it, you'll realize that it's something great. Sure, it may be risky— but risks can definitely take you to greener and better pastures. Good Luck!

# Conclusion

Thank you again for downloading this book!

I hope this book was able to help you learn how to earn passive income within 6 months - the easy way!

The next step is to put this information to use, and begin using the strategies provided to introduce passive income generation into your day to day life.
Finally, if you enjoyed this book, please take the time to share your thoughts and post a review.  It'd be greatly appreciated!

Thank you and good luck!

# Author

My name is Theeradech Thapanaphong and I have experience in many fields as Medical field, Astrology Field, Career Field, Outsource, and Consultant. I shared all my skill and experience to this book and we want to give my knowledge to all the audiences.